PARIS
THE CITY AT A GLA

GW00537976

Tour Montparnasse
Looming over low-rise Pari
high 1970s landmark is bac
See p010

Musée d'Orsay
Housed in Victor Laloux's 1900 Gare d'Orsay
and always thronged, this emblem of old Paris
has works by Rodin, Manet and Renoir.
1 rue de la Légion d'Honneur, 7ᵉ, T 4049 4814

Palais Garnier
Charles Garnier's ornate Second Empire
monument boasts a seven-tonne crystal
chandelier (that crushed an opera-goer in
1896) and Marc Chagall's 1964 ceiling art.
8 rue Scribe, 9ᵉ, T 08 9289 9090

Jardin des Tuileries
In the riverside gardens that connect the
Louvre and Place de la Concorde, the Jeu de
Paume gallery (1 place de la Concorde, 8ᵉ,
T 4703 1250) shows world-class photography.

Hôtel des Invalides
Now a military museum, this former soldiers'
hospice and convent, which dates from 1674,
was modified to house Napoleon Bonaparte's
superbly grand tomb under the dome.
Esplanade des Invalides, 7ᵉ, T 08 1011 3399

Eglise de la Trinité
Théodore Ballu's 1867 church was part of the
reorganisation of Paris under Haussmann.
Place d'Estienne d'Orves, 9ᵉ, T 4874 1277

Grand Palais
The vast glass-roofed exhibition hall built for
the 1900 Expo hosts art fairs including FIAC
and Monumenta, which lives up to its name.
*3 avenue du Général Eisenhower, 8ᵉ,
T 4413 1717*

INTRODUCTION
THE CHANGING FACE OF THE URBAN SCENE

It can be tempting to get nostalgic about Paris, to imagine there is still a corner where you'll catch a glimpse of Eugène de Rastignac, or stumble across a beatific Miles Davis en route to Club Saint-Germain. Yet, defying those who believe it to be nothing more than a beguiling relic, Paris surges ahead with major cultural projects, as fast-moving and trend-driven as any other digital-age capital.

Montmartre, recently fashionable, has settled into a gentrified calm, although it is still a dream for shopping and sightseeing. The *branché* district right now, where contemporary design spaces and independent boutiques cluster, is the Haut-Marais, especially the northern fringes and up into the 10th around post-seedy Rue du Faubourg Saint-Denis. The 11th, known for grungy nightlife, has become a hive of gastro innovation. Eventually, you may prefer to retire from the bobo bustle to more tranquil areas such as the 5th, the leafy 7th, and the bourgeois galleries of Saint-Germain. Equally good for slowing the pace are the fashion flagships and elite hotels and restaurants lining the wealthy boulevards of the Right Bank.

Plans for Le Grand Paris, a hugely ambitious extension of the tightly belted core, will see more change here than at any time since Haussmann, with large-scale urban projects undertaken, and the heart of the metropolis redesignated as one of several centres. For now, while you can still walk from the Eiffel Tower to Place de la Bastille and feel you've seen this elegant city, classic Paris lives.

ESSENTIAL INFO
FACTS, FIGURES AND USEFUL ADDRESSES

TOURIST OFFICE
25 rue des Pyramides, 1er
www.parisinfo.com

TRANSPORT
Airport transfer to city centre
RER line B trains depart regularly from
Charles de Gaulle Airport between 5am and
12am. The journey takes 25 to 35 minutes
www.aeroportsdeparis.fr
Car hire
Avis
T 08 2123 0760
www.avis.fr
Metro
Trains run from 5.30am until 1am, Sunday
to Thursday; and from 5.30am until 2am
on Fridays and Saturdays
www.ratp.fr
Taxi
Taxis G7
T 4127 6699
Travel Card
A carnet (10 metro/bus tickets) is €13.70

EMERGENCY SERVICES
Emergencies
T 112
24-hour pharmacy
Pharmacie Les Champs Dhéry
84 avenue des Champs-Élysées, 8e
T 4562 0241

EMBASSIES
British Embassy
35 rue du Faubourg Saint-Honoré, 8e
T 4451 3100
www.gov.uk/government/world/france
US Embassy
2 avenue Gabriel, 8e
T 4312 2222
france.usembassy.gov

POSTAL SERVICES
Post office
52 rue du Louvre, 1er
T 4028 1418
Shipping
UPS
T 08 2123 3877
www.ups.com

BOOKS
L'Architecture des Années 30 à Paris
by Jean-Marc Larbodière (Charles Massin)
Paris: de la Rue à la Galerie by Nicolas
Chenus and Samantha Longhi (Pyramyd)

WEBSITES
Art/Design
www.musee-orsay.fr
www.patrickseguin.com
Newspaper
www.lemonde.fr

EVENTS
Art Paris
www.artparis.fr
Maison & Objet
www.maison-objet.com
Nuit Blanche
www.nuitblanche.paris.fr

COST OF LIVING
**Taxi from Charles de Gaulle Airport
to city centre**
€50
Cappuccino
€3
Packet of cigarettes
€6
Daily newspaper
€2
Bottle of champagne
€80

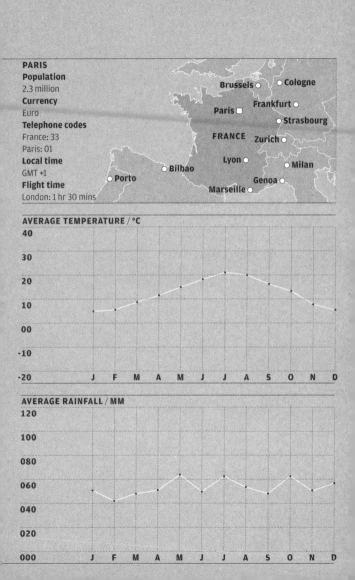

PARIS
Population
2.3 million
Currency
Euro
Telephone codes
France: 33
Paris: 01
Local time
GMT +1
Flight time
London: 1 hr 30 mins

Brussels ○   ○ Cologne

Frankfurt ○

Paris □

○ Strasbourg

FRANCE   Zurich ○

Lyon ○

○ Milan

○ Bilbao

Genoa ○

○ Porto

Marseille ○

AVERAGE TEMPERATURE / °C

40											
30											
20											
10											
00											
-10											
-20| J	F	M	A	M	J	J	A	S	O	N	D

AVERAGE RAINFALL / MM

120											
100											
080											
060											
040											
020											
000| J	F	M	A	M	J	J	A	S	O	N	D

NEIGHBOURHOODS

THE AREAS YOU NEED TO KNOW AND WHY

To help you navigate the city, we've chosen the most interesting districts (see below and the map inside the back cover) and colour-coded our featured venues, according to their location; those venues that are outside these areas are not coloured.

MONTMARTRE

Rising above the city, Montmartre remains aloof from the rest of Paris. Check into the tranquil Hôtel Particulier (see p022) and explore the cafés and restaurants lining Rue des Martyrs. Make a reservation for dinner at modern bistrot Le Pantruche (3 rue Victor Massé, 9e, T 4878 5560).

CANAL SAINT-MARTIN

The east-Paris bobo (bourgeois-bohème) crowd lingers beside the banks of this canal, along Rue de Marseille and Rue Beaurepaire. Stay at Le Citizen (96 quai de Jemmapes, 10e, T 8362 5550) for its watery views. To the east, in the 19th, the hipsters continue to push into Belleville.

CHAMPS-ÉLYSÉES

There is a slight stain of tackiness around the Champs-Élysées itself, but the area still has plenty to offer, including Pavillon Ledoyen (see p032), now the domain of Yannick Alléno, and contemporary luxury hotels such as La Maison Champs Élysées (8 rue Jean Goujon, 8e, T 4074 6465).

RÉPUBLIQUE/BASTILLE

Rue Oberkampf's legendary nightlife is not what it was, but the area has scrubbed up nicely, as bars such as Le Perchoir (see p031) lure hip fun-seekers. Thanks to Iñaki Aizpitarte of Le Châteaubriand (see p032), Bertrand Grébaut of Septime (see p052) and James Henry's Bones (see p030), the 11th is the zone for culinary discovery.

MARAIS

Fashion stores and art galleries, such as Gosserez (see p061) and S Bensimon (see p068), are dotted around Rue Debelleyme, Rue de Saintonge and Rue Charlot. At the northern edge, check out chic Argentinian steakhouse Anahi (see p040), and LO/A (see p094), a diverting thematic bookstore.

BEAUBOURG/LOUVRE

The Louvre (see p028) is an essential stop, despite its spirit-sapping vastness and the Dan Brown-devouring hordes. Don't miss out on its 2012 Department of Islamic Art, followed by lunch nearby at no-bookings udon noodle specialist Kunitoraya (5 rue Villedo, 1er, T 4703 0774).

SAINT-GERMAIN/QUARTIER LATIN

This smart neighbourhood is packed with galleries, cafés and shops, such as swish department store Le Bon Marché (24 rue de Sèvres, 7e, T 4439 8000), the new Ami shop (see p084) and high-design Hermès Sèvres (see p093). East along the river, Les Docks (see p076) is a creative focal point.

LES INVALIDES

Already lined with imposing monuments, this district can now boast Jean Nouvel's Musée du quai Branly (see p025); compare and contrast with the quartier's former highlight, the UNESCO Headquarters (see p012). Feast and then rest at Thoumieux (see p042), Jean-François Piège's splendid brasserie, restaurant and boutique hotel.

LANDMARKS
THE SHAPE OF THE CITY SKYLINE

Unlike Rome or Venice, Paris never has to live off its past for very long, because it always manages to reinvent itself. How it does this has a lot to do with the structure of the metropolis. Paris has retained the same shape for centuries by spreading out steadily from the diminutive island, today Île de la Cité, where the Parisii, a community of Celtic fisherfolk, settled in 250BC. As its population increased, the city expanded in concentric circles, now stretching as far as the Périphérique ring road. Chloé-clad commuters lead *Desperate Housewives*-on-the-Seine lifestyles in the leafy western suburbs, such as Saint-Cloud and Neuilly, while the underclass re-enacts *La Haine* in 1950s hellholes beyond the ring road.

Contemporary Paris consists of more than two million people living inside the 9.7km diameter of the Périphérique, with Île de la Cité still at its centre. The good news is that, whereas sprawling cities such as Los Angeles can afford to neglect their architecture, land is so precious within the unofficial boundary of Paris that Parisians strive to preserve theirs. And the city puts almost as much effort into building new monuments as it does into cherishing old ones – think of Henri IV ordering the construction of an expensive residential district, the Marais, around Place des Vosges in the early 1600s. All of which means that not only is navigation easy, but the landmarks that line the way are worth lingering over.
For full addresses, see Resources.

Tour Montparnasse

The redevelopment of the down-at-heel area around Gare Montparnasse in the early 1960s was, by and large, a piece of inspired city planning. Jean Dubuisson's scheme included a monumental slab of a residential block, with a wonderful gridded curtain wall. Unfortunately, it also allowed for this 210m-tall totem pole in the middle of low-rise Paris. Together with the high-rise buildings along the Seine, which were commissioned under Georges Pompidou's prime ministership, this tower, finished in 1973, is back in vogue with city opinion-formers. On the 56th floor, there is an observation terrace, a champagne bar and a glamorous restaurant, Ciel de Paris (T 4064 7764; reservations only), designed by Noé Duchaufour-Lawrance.
33 avenue du Maine, 15ᵉ, T 4538 5256,
www.tourmontparnasse56.com

Grande Arche de la Défense

The proposal to construct a new business district to the west of the centre was first advanced in the early 1950s, but it was this 1989 landmark that fixed La Défense in the popular imagination. The hollowed-out cube reaches up to 110m high, and the stark, almost graphic lines of its facades are emphasised by the use of glazing and white Carrara marble. The creation of a Danish duo, architect Johann Otto von Spreckelsen and engineer Erik Reitzel, the arch is scaled on both sides by lifts, which provide panoramic views of greater Paris, as well as down the axis of Champs-Élysées (sadly the roof is currently closed to the public). Nearby is French architect Christian de Portzamparc's angular Tour Granite, which was built for Groupe Société Générale and completed in 2008.

1 parvis de la Défense

UNESCO Headquarters

When this complex was finished in 1958, writer Lewis Mumford dismissed it as a 'museum of antiquated modernities'. Even now, in the eyes of some critics, the building hasn't really recovered from this withering assessment. Conceived by a trio of celebrated architects, Marcel Breuer, Pier Luigi Nervi and Bernard Zehrfuss, it was one of the first major modern works to be constructed in the centre of the city. All the same, the seven-storey, Y-shaped office block (left), resting on 72 concrete stilts, has become a Paris landmark, and the congress hall, with its concertina-like structure, has come to be seen as a masterpiece of modern design. Picasso, Miró, Tàpies and Le Corbusier were just some of the artists commissioned to create pieces for the complex; in 1995, Japanese architect Tadao Ando added an exquisite small meditation space to the site.

7 place de Fontenoy, 7ᵉ, www.unesco.org

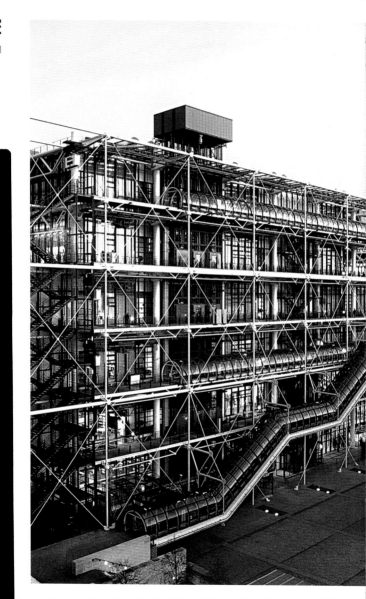

Centre Pompidou

The moment when architecture became icon can be traced to 1977, when Richard Rogers, Renzo Piano and Gianfranco Franchini's technical and functional tour de force was unveiled. One of France's most visited venues, the Pompidou can appear untidy, but it is a classic example of a building as city symbol. It houses the Musée National d'Art Moderne, a library and a musical research centre. Seven storeys of glass, steel and concrete are encased in an exoskeleton of colour-coded pipes – green for plumbing, blue for climate control, electrical wires in yellow, and red for communication. In 2010, the Pompidou opened an outpost in Metz (T 03 8715 3939), for which architects Shigeru Ban and Jean de Gastines came up with a hexagonal plan enveloped in an undulating marquee-style wood roof. *Place Georges Pompidou, 4ᵉ, T 4478 1233, www.centrepompidou.fr*

HOTELS
WHERE TO STAY AND WHICH ROOMS TO BOOK

The deluxe room count in Paris, one of the world's great hotel cities, just keeps rising. Over the past few years, big-hitter Asian brands like Mandarin Oriental, Shangri-La and Peninsula (opposite) have joined the grandes dames; Plaza Athénée (25 avenue Montaigne, 8e, T 5367 6665) has quietly acquired a new wing to compete.

Beyond the bells and whistles, attractive choices are appearing in upcoming areas. Hôtel Paradis (see p018) and its sibling, Hôtel Panache (1 rue Geoffroy-Marie, 9e, T 4770 8587), have interiors by Dorothée Meilichzon. Hôtel Edgar (31 rue d'Alexandrie, 2e, T 4041 0519) has a decent seafood restaurant and rooms created by an arty coterie. A food-led berth between Oberkampf and Bastille, Auberge Flora (44 boulevard Richard-Lenoir, 11e, T 4700 5277) was designed by Simone&Hug. Among other gourmet choices is the super-sleek Hôtel de Nell (see p053), by architect Jean-Michel Wilmotte.

There's minimalist cool out in the 20th at Philippe Starck's Mama Shelter (109 rue de Bagnolet, 20e, T 4348 4848), and at Le Citizen (96 quai de Jemmapes, 10e, T 8362 5550), on Canal Saint-Martin. In the Marais, Jules & Jim (see p019) and Le Pavillon de la Reine (28 place des Vosges, 3e, T 4029 1919) remain perennial favourites. Alternatively, head for the leafy Montmartre hills, to the charming Hôtel Particulier (see p022), or, nearby in South Pigalle, Maison Souquet (10 rue de Bruxelles, 9e), designed by Jacques Garcia. *For full addresses and room rates, see Resources.*

The Peninsula

Stupendously retooled for the 21st century, this historic pile glitters with hand-applied gold leaf and gleams with marble. Hoping to lure and secure China's new tourist class, the Peninsula serves congee alongside the croissants at breakfast, and the lavish LiLi restaurant (T 5812 6750) presents Sichuan and Cantonese dishes beneath giant silk tassels and an opera headdress twinkling with crystal. The rooms (Premier Suite, above) are low-key, especially considering the luxe elsewhere, featuring leather art deco-style headboards crafted by London artist Helen Murray, offset by high-tech lighting, entertainment run by tablet and mirrored bathrooms. The produce-led French cuisine in the top-floor L'Oiseau Blanc (T 5812 6730) is perfectly pitched. *19 avenue Kléber, 16e, T 5812 2888, paris.peninsula.com*

Hôtel Paradis

Cool, even sexy, not to mention great value and within walking distance of the Gare du Nord, Hôtel Paradis is already on the map for hip young Brits. Independent hoteliers Julie and Adrien Gloaguen took a gamble on this gritty *microquartier*, now booming with a dozen or so lively bars and bistrots. Dorothée Meilichzon has brought warmth and substance to the 38 rooms through an *au courant* design that melds colour, textiles and patterned wallpaper – checks, florals, swirly clouds – incorporating the property's original brickwork, parquet and mouldings. The rooms (301, above) are big, if lacking in storage space, which, given the price, is no great loss. Breakfast is minimal; the charming welcome is what makes this place such a keeper.

41 rue des Petites Écuries, 10ᵉ,
T 4523 0822, www.hotelparadisparis.com

Hôtel Jules & Jim

Built virtually from scratch on the site of an old precious-metal workshop, Jules & Jim is modish but not overweeningly trendy – it has its arty moments and a pretty cool bar, but is an affordable and friendly base for everyone. The five-year conversion, undertaken with architects Heinrich Fitger and interior designers Atome Associés, has been a labour of love for the owners, Geoffroy Sciard and Antoine Brault. There are five styles of accommodation, including diminutive pods with glowing bauxite walls and rooftop views, and more conventional rooms in a separate building. Drinks and breakfast are served in the former carriage house, decorated with 1950s-style tables, settees from Red Edition and chairs by Anégil. *11 rue des Gravilliers, 3ᵉ, T 4454 1313, www.hoteljuleseljim.com*

Hotel Molitor

The blue, blue outdoor swimming pool, to which everything else at Molitor bows, is sensational – can the idea of the 'urban resort' ever have come into its own so charmingly? There's a fascinating history here. The art deco glass panels are relics from the complex's long stint as a *piscine municipale* (there is also a 1930s indoor pool), and decoration remains from when the building was squatted and festooned with graffiti. Out in the 16th, it might be remote in terms of footfall, yet the Molitor roof terrace is a scene in the summer, and contemporary art events are a draw. In contrast to the shock yellow of the public areas (opposite), the 124 rooms are calm and understated; the three Hublot Suites (above) have jolly porthole windows.

13 rue Nungesser et Coli, 16ᵉ,
T 5607 0850, www.mltr.fr

Hôtel Particulier Montmartre

Despite the swarms of tourists en route to Sacré-Coeur, and the area's slow but steady gentrification, pockets of the Montmartre district retain an atmosphere unmatched anywhere else in Paris. On stylish Avenue Junot, the discreet Particulier occupies a 19th-century townhouse, once owned by the Hermès family, and looks on to gardens by Louis Benech. The filmmaker Morgane Rousseau turned it into a five-suite hotel with a cinematic theme that incorporates works by French artists; reserve Poèmes et Chapeaux (opposite) or the Rideau de Cheveux Suite, which features portrait photography by Natacha Lesueur. Art happenings are the norm: look for Sophie Comtet Kouyaté's Saint-Denis portraits, 'Les Dionysiennes', all throughout 2015. *23 avenue Junot, 18ᵉ, T 5341 8140, www.hotel-particulier-montmartre.com*

24 HOURS

SEE THE BEST OF THE CITY IN JUST ONE DAY

Owing to Paris' petite size relative to, say, London, the city smiles on intrepid visitors who want to explore both sides of the Seine. For brunch at weekends, try the anglophile affair at Le Bal Café (6 impasse de la Défense, 18e, T 4470 7551), the anything-goes menu at The Peninsula (see p017) or, for hot chocolate, champagne and madeleines, the Sunday spread at Un Dimanche à Paris (4 cour du Commerce Saint-André, 6e, T 5681 1818). Alternatively, a gourmet outing could well start on Rue des Martyrs, winding down from Montmartre; pause for *lèche-vitrine* at Pâtisserie des Martyrs (No 22, 9e, T 7118 2470) and continue on Rue du Faubourg-Montmartre for food shopping around Montorgueil. You could then go west to the Bois de Boulogne, for lunch by the pool at Molitor (see p020), followed by a look at the Fondation Louis Vuitton (see p070), just one of the art behemoths on the must-see list, which include Musée du quai Branly (opposite) on the Left Bank, and the raw spaces of Palais de Tokyo (see p026) directly across the river.

Much of what's exciting at night is concentrated around Bastille, Oberkampf and Ménilmontant, so head out east for drinks at the dinky La Buvette (see p048), *en plein air* at Le Perchoir (see p031), or for dinner at a hip-yet-refined bistrot such as Bones (see p030). After hours, the nightclub Le Baron (6 avenue Marceau, 8e) has still got it, and attracts an arty, monied, sometimes louche crowd. *For full addresses, see Resources.*

10.00 Musée du quai Branly

Resembling a long footbridge in a forest of green – a vertical garden by Patrick Blanc covers one wall – Jean Nouvel's Musée du quai Branly was opened in 2006 to exhibit non-Western art (including contemporary indigenous pieces) from Africa, Asia, the Americas and Oceania. Taken as a whole, it might be overwhelming; instead, focus on, say, Siberian shamanism brought alive via multimedia, Aboriginal bark paintings as collected by Karel Kupka in the 1960s, or ikat textiles, which are significant not only in South-East Asia but also in India, Syria and Yemen. The threads and themes, as well as 'transversals' that bring together the likes of musical instruments or textiles from sub-Saharan Africa, offer rewarding ways of looking at world culture.
*37 quai Branly, 7e, T 5661 7000,
www.quaibranly.fr*

12.30 Palais de Tokyo
Extended in 2012, so it now reaches down to the Seine, Palais de Tokyo is a must for its surveys of contemporary art, and its architecture – a 22,000 sq m labyrinth of concrete chambers and lofty alcoves. Anne Lacaton and Jean-Philippe Vassal took a minimalist approach to the renovation, freeing up space and revealing the vast proportions. In some of the rooms, it can feel as if you're entering a no-go area, so unsignposted and unrefined is the finish. As many of the artworks are disruptive of normative seeing, the experience can be thrillingly disorienting; the venue's fabric is also subject to intervention. Afterwards have lunch at Monsieur Blue (above; T 4720 9047), designed by Joseph Dirand. The museum opens at noon; closed Tuesdays. *13 avenue du Président Wilson, 16e, T 8197 3588, www.palaisdetokyo.com*

16.00 Department of Islamic Art
Inaugurated in 2012, the undulating roof
of some 2,350 triangular panels in gold
and silver aluminium mesh that occupies
Cour Visconti shields the Louvre's Islamic
art treasures. Its deliberately cloak-like
quality saves the structure from what
architect Mario Bellini, who designed the
gallery with Rudy Ricciotti, says would
have been 'embarrassing cross-pollination
with the 18th-century character of the
palace'. The illusion of suspension and
fluidity gives the project a lightness and
unexpectedness in keeping with the
museum's prior contemporary flourish,
IM Pei's 1989 glass pyramid. The Islamic
collection spans 1,300 years and three
continents, covering ceramics, glassware,
textiles, calligraphy and precious metals.
*Louvre, 1 place du Carrousel, 1er,
T 4020 5317, www.louvre.fr*

19.30 Bones

The ingenuity of James Henry's food, and his dedication to making his own cheeses, charcuterie, butter and bread, belie the tiny single-file kitchen here at Bones. The rough-hewn dining room, with its street lamps, peeling walls and unfancy furniture, is relaxed and convivial, lubricated by a 1970s rock soundtrack and a thrilling list of drinks. Book about a week ahead for the €55 dinner menu, which might involve scallop and lovage salad, radishes with ricotta and *bagna càuda*, wild venison or *ris de veau*. The no-reservations bar area (above), which has high stools as well as concrete banquettes and window seats, means that even the most disorganised can drop in for a bite to eat, a drink and to partake of good vibes.

43 rue Godefroy Cavaignac, 11ᵉ,
T 09 8075 3208, www.bonesparis.com

22.00 Le Perchoir

This rooftop hangout has a holiday feel, and is best enjoyed on a school night, when it's nonetheless advisable to turn up early or late to beat the crowds. The restaurant proper serves Provençal small plates, and brings the 400 sq m *terrasse* indoors via wrought-iron and wood tables, mismatched chairs, tiling and industrial windows. Go alfresco with a pisco sour and a pile of duck confit tacos in summer, for 360-degree views from Père Lachaise to Sacré-Coeur. Elsewhere in the neighbourhood, the tiny L'Entrée des Artistes (T 09 5099 6711), although grouchily staffed, does some of the classiest late-night cocktails in Paris, and Aux Deux Amis (T 5830 3813) is a natural wine bar and bistrot that heaves with thirtysomethings on Friday nights. *14 rue Crespin du Gast, 11ᵉ, T 4806 1848, www.leperchoir.fr*

URBAN LIFE
CAFÉS, RESTAURANTS, BARS AND NIGHTCLUBS

The *bistronomie* scene that restored the city's culinary mettle is into its third decade, and Septime (see p052), Le Châteaubriand (129 avenue Parmentier, 11e, T 4357 4595) and Gregory Marchand's much-lauded Frenchie (5-6 rue du Nil, 2e, T 4039 9619) offer some of the most dynamic dining in Paris. Their alumni, such as Simone Tondo at Roseval (see p047), are establishing their own informal, produce-savvy styles. Biodynamic and natural wines from small operations in France and Italy are the rule at these establishments.

At the high end, Yannick Alléno now shakes the pans at Pavillon Ledoyen (8 avenue Dutuit, 8e, T 5305 1001), and Pascal Barbot's Asian-tinged vegcentric menu at L'Astrance (4 rue Beethoven, 16e, T 4050 8440) draws visiting chefs. The definitive bistrot is arguably Paul Bert (18 rue Paul Bert, 11e, T 4372 2401), which has a seafood sibling next door, L'Ecailler du Bistrot (No 22, T 4372 7677).

Hot venues in the 11th – the must-visit arrondissement for food-lovers – include the casual Le Servan (32 rue Saint-Maur, 11e, T 5528 5182), run by ex-L'Astrance chef Tatiana Levha and her sister Katia, and Clown Bar (114 rue Amelot, 11e, T 4355 8735), the Saturne (see p039) team's takeover of a zany century-old annexe of the Cirque d'Hiver. In the Marais, SŌMA (13 rue de Saintonge, 3e, T 09 8182 5351) is a bustling izakaya. And the BBQ trend has arrived in Pigalle, at the aptly named Flesh (25 rue de Douai, 9e, T 4281 2193).
For full addresses, see Resources.

Café Artcurial

For this Italian restaurant, a concession of auction house Artcurial, designer Charles Zana drew inspiration from Gio Ponti and Ettore Sottsass, while respecting the 19th-century fabric of Hôtel Marcel Dassault, which houses Artcurial's showrooms and bookstore (don't miss). Entry is via the salon, furnished with sofas and chairs of Zana's creation and diamond-patterned walls; the 'orangery' has a glass canopy and 1960s pendants; and restaurateur Enrico Einaudi presides hospitably over the marble bar. The food is plated with élan – a squiggle of sauce here, a copper pan there – and centres on Piedmontese cuisine, so there is *vitello tonnato* and *tajarin* pasta with ceps and sage. Wines are Italian, as are most of the staff.
7 rond-point des Champs-Élysées, 8ᵉ,
T 5376 3934, www.artcurial.com/cafe

Le Sergent Recruteur

Like many hip young tables in Paris, this Île Saint-Louis restaurant attracts diners with a fixed-price menu (lunch from €48, more at night with matched wines). But there the comparison ends. Chef Antonin Bonnet is no ingénue, and his desire is to shrink the supply chain, directly sourcing Breton lobster, rare-bred meat, heritage vegetables and wild herbs. The knives, the wood floor and even the Berkel Marzocco coffee machine were designed according to Bonnet's wishes. Jaime Hayón's striking decor of marble, masks and mirrors, and an Aubusson-style tapestry, has helped to transform this antiquated building into an *haute* destination. The wine list roams around exciting small producers in France, Spain, Germany and Greece.
41 rue Saint-Louis en l'Île, 4ᵉ, T 4354 7542, www.lesergentrecruteur.fr

Compagnie des Vins Surnaturels
This civilised hang-out is a bit of a tease,
namewise. The 400-bin wine list leans
away from low-sulphite *vins naturels*;
in fact, the foremost expert among the
various owners is a big Bordeaux dealer.
Well-heeled thirty- and fortysomething
Parisians saunter in after work, settling
into upholstered armchairs and ikat-print
sofas chosen by young French designer
Dorothée Meilichzon, and spending from
€20 to several hundred euros on Bordeaux
reds, whites from Burgundy and the Loire,
and interesting cuvées from the south,
Italy, even Israel and Uruguay. Excellent
entry-level wines include the Louis Jadot
Couvent des Jacobins burgundy and the
Laporte Terre des Anges sancerre. Food
is rather secondary, so keep it simple
with a cheese platter or the bellota ham.
7 rue Lobineau, 6ᵉ, T 09 5490 2020,
www.compagniedesvinssurnaturels.com

Clamato

Fans of Septime (see p052) are all aglow about this next-door offshoot, which has a looser, later vibe, a no-reservations policy, and a globetrotting, ocean-going menu quite unlike more traditional Paris seafood joints. The cabin-esque interior features parquet bricks on the floor that continue up the side of the bar, bench seating, wood tables and a pine-clad ceiling. Arrive when the doors open at 7pm, or after 9.30pm, to avoid the crowds, and order to share. Start with clams – ask your server for the *plus fines* – and perhaps a living crevette (very Noma), followed by ceviche of grey mullet, tuna sashimi with chives and *umezu* plum vinegar, and marinated sardines. The puddings are fantastic too: leave room for the damson clafoutis with basil sorbet. *80 rue du Charonne, 11^e, T 4372 7453, www.septime-charonne.fr*

Saturne

Chef Sven Chartier, just 24 years old at the time, opened Saturne with the sommelier Ewen Lemoigne in 2010. The pared-back, Scandi-style interior features undressed tables, Jean Louis Iratzoki's felt- and wool-covered oak 'Laia' chairs, stone walls and an open kitchen, illuminated by a giant skylight and light fittings by Serge Mouille and Céline Wright. The €40 lunch menu and €65 'surprise' dinner of six courses deploy impeccably sourced ingredients in dishes such as gilt-head bream and Utah Beach oyster with pear granita and Savagnin vinegar, and lobster with thyme, cauliflower and lemon. *Vins naturels* from the Loire, Auvergne, Languedoc and Savoie are ambrosial, especially with Lemoigne's guidance. Saturne is closed at weekends. *17 rue Notre Dame des Victoires, 2ᵉ, T 4260 3190, www.saturne-paris.fr*

Anahi

Like a game of gastronomic Monopoly, some 40 neighbouring buildings along La Jeune Rue have been reborn by designers of the calibre of Patricia Urquiola, Jasper Morrison and Ingo Maurer, and top chefs and restaurateurs are moving in. Anahi, the only existing restaurant on the roster, has had its own facelift. Maud Bury has reworked the former butcher's by touching up cracked tiles with golden copper leaf, hanging gilded 'hams' in the rear (above) and sheathing chairs in brass. Candlelit, it all looks wonderful. Top-drawer French produce is Anahi's secret ingredient, along with Argentine chef Osvaldo Lupis. Start with empanadas, corn *humitas* or ceviche, before a *bife chuleta*, aka *côte de boeuf*, to share, along with a biodynamic Priorat.
49 rue Volta, 3ᵉ, T 4887 8824,
www.anahirestaurant.fr

Le 6 Paul Bert

Bertrand Auboyneau's Le Bistrot Paul Bert is all about *steak frites* and *blanquette de veau*, but its next-door offshoot heads in a more modern direction, its semi-open kitchen sending out small plates with a Scandi or even British bent: monkfish liver comes with chard and nettle, mackerel is served with pickles, and desserts are fresh, not sugary, and play with temperature and texture. *Le patron*, who wrote the book on the contemporary Paris bistrot (literally: copies are on sale here), is evangelistic about natural wines – look for producers such as Pierre Overnoy and Dard & Ribo. The decoration is jaunty and undone, with nostalgic posters, and light fittings made from wine bottles or cutlery. It attracts a chic crowd, and the room is alive until late, with a second sitting about 10pm.
6 rue Paul Bert, 11ᵉ, T 4379 1432

Brasserie Thoumieux
Since the relaunch by Thierry Costes, whose family is behind so many of Paris' see-and-be-seen destinations, and chef Jean-François Piège, this venue is abuzz again, offering a snapshot of the well-heeled habitués of the 7th. The upstairs restaurant has two Michelin stars, and there's a refined 14-room hotel (T 4705 7900) with interiors by India Mahdavi.
79 rue Saint-Dominique, 7ᵉ, T 4705 4975

Stern Caffè

This Italian all-dayer in the 19th-century retail arcade Passage des Panoramas is a collaboration between the Alajmo family, famed for the highly respected restaurant Le Calandre in Padua, Italy, and Philippe Starck. As is his wont, the designer has deployed stuffed coyotes, an ex-rabbit, hats as lampshades, and a wall of curios, and somehow it actually gels with the Cordoba leather walls and parquet floors of this former engraver's shop (note the sign outside). The offering is excellent, from the first espresso of the day, served in golden Stern coffee cups, to Campari spritz and *cicchetti* for the *apéro* before cep risotto with white truffles and cream, or seabass carpaccio with caviar. There's an extensive list of sparkling whites.
47 passage des Panoramas, 2e,
T 7543 6310, www.caffestern.com

Café Kitsuné

Le Palais-Royal is a narrow slice of prime fashion real estate – Acne, Marc Jacobs and Stella McCartney moved into its 17th-century colonnades a few years ago. Café Kitsuné is perfect for a retail pitstop, fun and frothy and popular with the cool kids, much like the French/Japanese record label and streetwear brand it sprang from. Coffee is brewed from sustainable Daterra beans from Brazil; order with a fox-shaped biscuit (*kitsune* is Japanese for 'fox') or a slice of gluten-free cake. On hotter days, try the iced *matcha* (green tea). Kitsuné merchandise (bags and caps) is on sale; sadly, the Jean-Philippe Delhomme fox painting is not. The parquet, mouldings and signage are relics from the premises' former incarnation as a textile workshop.
51 galerie de Montpensier, 1ᵉ, T 4015 6231, www.kitsune.fr

Eclectic

Fabienne and Philippe Amzalak are well known among the design community for Ma Cocotte (T 4151 7000) in Saint-Ouen fleamarket, a weekend brunch favourite. Their latest trick is this 160-cover business restaurant with a brasserie feel, created by Tom Dixon and Design Research Studio in the Centre Commercial Beaugrenelle, which opened in the late 1970s. Dixon has given us a tribute to that decade, using lots of concrete, hexagonal motifs and sculptural furniture and banquettes, with booths overlooking the Seine. The feel is loungey, glamorous and international, and the all-day menu follows suit, with tuna *chirashi*, Venetian carpaccio and steak au poivre. The Taittinger Brut served by the glass is another reason to drop by.
2 rue Linois, 15e, T 7736 7000,
www.restauranteclectic.fr

Roseval

This is one of the most rewarding of the prix-fixe bistros, and Roseval's pared-back decor – brick, concrete, whitewash, fresh flowers and covetable ceramics – is in tune with the contemporary cuisine and natural wine list. Michael Greenwold left to open his *haute* diner, The Sunken Chip (T 5326 7446), but Simone Tondo is doing just fine, pleasing allcomers with his light, delicate cooking. In summer, the set menu might feature frothy soup of clams and courgette; marinated mackerel served with fresh cheese; *encornet, pommes de terre, algues*, an earthy take on grilled squid; scallops with raspberries; and pigeon and chard purée. If you haven't booked a table, ring the same day to turn up for second service. Closed weekends. *1 rue d'Eupatoria, 20°, T 09 5356 2414, www.roseval.fr*

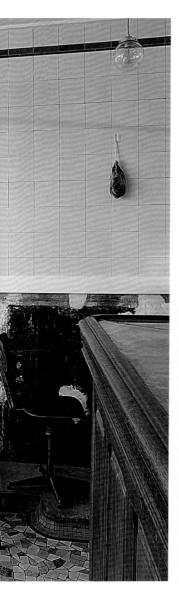

La Buvette

This miniscule wine bar with its broken tile flooring, 1930s oak counter and just a couple of tables represents much that is current in Parisian gastronomy. Camille Fourmont, previously at the refined tapas and wine bar Le Dauphin (T 5528 7888), operates in a lo-fi, even old-fashioned style, although her choice of alimentation is anything but, offering elite products at non-scary prices. There's no kitchen as such, just a dinky prep area and a top-quality ham slicer; listed on the blackboard (actually a mirror) are small plates such as duck magret with Bordier raspberry butter, goat's cheeses marinated with green pepper and vanilla, and Trikalinos sardines with yuzu vinegar. Wine comes courtesy of Sarnin-Berrux in Burgundy and Muriel Giudicelli in Corsica, and the beer hails from the local Goutte d'Or brewery. Look out for the neon sign.
67 rue Saint-Maur, 11ᵉ, T 09 8356 9411

Chambelland

Gluten-free cuisine is big in Paris right now, and Chambelland is its most accomplished exponent. Entrepreneur Nathaniel Doboin and baker Thomas Teffri-Chambelland's watchwords are 'wellbeing and pleasure', and their commitment inspired them to set up their own mill and carry out months of research into flour (the winner was rice flour). All bread is kneaded and baked in-house, including the amazing five-grain loaf. Take a place at one of the unfussy tables, indoors or out, for a lunch of salad or vegetable soup, coffee and a handful of little *chouquette* pastries. On the deli shelves are homemade biscuits and exotic juices. The square-slices logo was created by the H5 collective (known for their music videos for Röyksopp and Air).
14 rue Ternaux, 11ᵉ, T 4355 0730,
www.chambelland.com

Le Mary Celeste

There is much that is welcoming about Le Mary Celeste, and the patient staff will find you a perch when it's busy (it's always busy) and chat even when the pressure's on. Plus, it occupies a premium position on a street corner, and has expansive windows and a sociable hexagonal bar centre stage. Kick into evening mode with a potent cocktail, such as the Marquee Moon, consisting of Beefeater gin, vermouth del Professore, pear, vanilla and absinthe, or a glass of Jacques Selosse fizz. Haan Palcu-Chang's adventurous menu changes daily, usually featuring oysters in season, and perhaps a veal ragout with jalapeños and polenta. The owners run nearby Candelaria (see p054) and Glass (T 09 8072 9883) in the 9th, both beloved of the party crowd.
1 rue Commines, 3ᵉ, T 09 8072 9883, www.lemaryceleste.com

Septime

Chef Bertrand Grébaut formerly cooked at L'Arpège (T 4705 0906) with Alain Passard, a 'natural' chef who inspired Noma and the New Nordics. Now he serves brilliant *bistronomie* near Bastille in his low-key, buzzy dining room, which has a farmhouse feel thanks to the rough-plastered walls, weathered tables and oxidised mirrors, and features an iron spiral staircase and vintage bell-jar pendant lights. Simply request either 'red' or 'white' for your aperitif, divulge any food intolerances, and the rest is decided for you. The €65 carte blanche menu makes the most of what's in season, in dishes such as cod with asparagus and grilled nasturtium leaves or duck with yellow beetroot. The modish desserts avoid pastry and cream. *80 rue de Charonne, 11ᵉ, T 4367 3829, www.septime-charonne.fr*

Hôtel de Nell

Purveyor of niche local spirits such as Cîroc vodka, Citadelle gin and old-school Suze, the small, sleek bar (above) in Hôtel de Nell can be quite fun, depending on the scene in its destination restaurant, La Régalade Conservatoire, for which it is the holding area. The *bistronomique* menu is courtesy of early adopter Bruno Doucel, who took over the first Régalade in the 14th in 2004, and is served on bespoke Bernardaud and Christofle tableware. Architect Jean-Michel Wilmotte spent two years turning this former residential site facing the original Paris Conservatoire into a hotel, stripping away everything except the facade and a listed staircase, and designing the elegant interiors, including vast Japanese baths, each carved from a single block of marble. *7-9 rue du Conservatoire, 9ᵉ, T 4483 8360, www.hoteldenell.com*

INSIDER'S GUIDE

ALPHA SIDIBE, STUDIO MANAGER

Guinea-born Alpha Sidibe lives in the Marais and works at Christian Louboutin. 'Paris mixes tradition and nostalgia with cool,' he says. 'There is great architecture but it keeps a human dimension – your *quartier* feels like a village.' Indeed, many of his favourite venues are local, including concept store/café The Broken Arm (12 rue Perrée, 3ᵉ, T 4461 5360) and 13 Bonaparte (2 bis rue de Normandie, 3ᵉ, T 4271 8315), for quality menswear, while Café La Perle (78 rue Vieille du Temple, 3ᵉ, T 4272 6993), popular with the fashion set, could be his second home, and Candelaria (52 rue de Saintonge, 3ᵉ, T 4274 4128) is a 'Parisian speakeasy behind a Mexican kitchen'.

When he has the time, Sidibe heads to *la banlieue* to Galerie Thaddaeus Ropac (69 avenue du Général Leclerc, Pantin, T 5589 0110), a contemporary art space in an old ironworks. He also likes the photography at Galerie d'en Face (7 rue Paul-Louis Courier, 7ᵉ, T 4439 9456) on the Left Bank. On an evening out, he often dines at Pamela Popo (15 rue François Miron, 4ᵉ, T 4274 1465) – 'named after the Gainsbourg song and run by a dynamic team' – or Les Nautes (1 quai des Célestins, 4ᵉ, T 4274 5953), by the river. Then it's drinks at La Jaja (56 rue d'Argout, 2ᵉ, T 09 5212 4101) before Silencio (142 rue Montmartre, 2ᵉ), an arts club co-designed by David Lynch that opens to all after midnight, or Maxim's (3 rue Royale, 8ᵉ, T 4265 2794), for 'chic late-night parties in a belle époque setting'.

For full addresses, see Resources.

ART AND DESIGN
GALLERIES, STUDIOS AND PUBLIC SPACES

The art scene in Paris has always leaned towards the highbrow, and it is perhaps becoming more so as it internationalises, with dealers such as Galerie Kreo (opposite) and Carpenters Workshop Gallery (54 rue de la Verrerie, 4e, T 4278 8092) maintaining premises in both London and the French capital. Scandinavian art is championed by Galerie Maria Wettergren (18 rue Guénégaud, 6e, T 4329 1960), and Triode (28 rue Jacob, 6e, T 4329 4005) represents US makers.

Midcentury French design remains as significant and covetable as ever, with Pascal Cuisinier (see p060) and Patrick Seguin (see p065) devoting essential shows to the stellar makers. In terms of the contemporary, the line between furniture and art has become more blurred than ever, at showrooms like Gosserez (see p061), S Bensimon (see p068) and Galerie BSL (23 rue Charlot, 3e, T 4478 9414), where Noé Duchaufour-Lawrance's sinuous Corian wave functions as a display device. All these are clustered in the Haut-Marais, providing a snapshot of an invigorating hybrid creativity.

Fondation Louis Vuitton (see p070) is the most talked-about public arrival, along with the reopened Musée Picasso (5 rue de Thorigny, 3e, T 8556 0036), which took double the time and euros to restore than expected, and now has 37 galleries. Out of town, the contemporary collides with history at the Palace of Versailles (see p064) in the form of Studio Bouroullec's graceful installation. *For full addresses, see Resources.*

Galerie Kreo

Seeing itself as a 'research laboratory', Kreo is dedicated to artistic exploration in design. Opened in 1999 by Clémence and Didier Krzentowski, it has secured exclusive rights to an impressive selection of limited-edition furniture, objects and lighting by leading creatives including Wieki Somers, Martin Szekely and Jasper Morrison. The Krzentowskis have a fluid arrangement with their stable, accepting that development takes time, and curate first-rate exhibitions. 'Techniques Mixtes, Dimensions Variables' (above) grouped Hella Jongerius' 'Swatch' table with Ronan and Erwan Bouroullec's 'Objets Lumineux', Alessandro Mendini's 'Tabouret Enigma' stool and Pierre Charpin's 'Ignotus Nomen' vase. Open Tuesday to Saturday. *31 rue Dauphine, 6ᵉ, T 5310 2300, www.galeriekreo.fr*

Vallois

Championing the New Realists, as well as emerging talent, this gallery has racked up a quarter of a century in Saint-Germain-des-Prés. It represents Jacques Villeglé, famed for his Lettrist and poster art from the 1950s on; sculptor and painter Niki de Saint Phalle; and Swiss Dadaist Jean Tinguely. Contemporary artists who have been granted solo shows are Americans Paul McCarthy and Jeff Mills, erstwhile YBA Keith Tyson, and French counterparts Alain Bublex and Gilles Barbier. There is also a fine publishing arm – Vallios' 2012 monograph on Tinguely includes pieces unseen for 50 years. The gallery recently took on the estate of pop art painter Alain Jacquet, while Virginie Yassef's 'Au Milieu du Crétacé' (above) was a 2014 highlight.
36 rue de Seine, 6ᵉ, T 4634 6107, www.galerie-vallois.com

Galerie Pascal Cuisinier

Among Rue de Seine's specialist stores is this showroom devoted to midcentury French furniture design. Pascal Cuisinier started off trading at the Saint-Ouen fleamarket, specialising in pieces dating from the 1930s to the 1960s. He then took time out to study, returning in 2006 to promote graduates of the École Nationale Supérieure des Arts Décoratifs, such as René-Jean Caillette, Pierre Guariche and Joseph-André Motte, and members of the 1950s Atelier des Recherches Plastiques, so expect plenty of folded plywood, latex foam and metal tubing. The gallery hosts well-researched exhibitions that rotate a few times a year, featuring pieces such as André Simard's 1955 sideboard and Gérard Guermonprez's 1958 chair (both above).
13 rue de Seine, 6ᵉ, T 4354 3461,
www.galeriepascalcuisinier.com

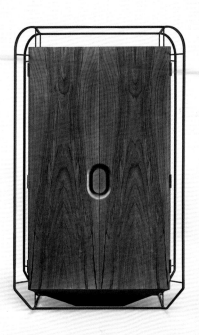

Galerie Gosserez

Marie-Bérangère Gosserez launched her showroom in 2010 to champion a group of makers for whom the design/art boundary is somewhat flexible. It is a blank canvas, sparsely filled with limited editions, many by up-and-coming French talent, from the furniture in beechwood and sustainable Zelfo by Elise Gabriel, to lighting by Julie Pfligersdorffer and Vaulot & Dyèvre, and sculptural pieces by Grégoire de Lafforest, whose 'Exo' range (wardrobe, above) was inspired by exoskeletons (his 'Cage Archibird' table segues into full-on art territory). There might also be handmade tables in burnt hazel and oak by Valentin Loellmann from Germany, or photography by Korean Heewon Kim. The fascinating selection is a great overview of the scene. *3 rue Debelleyme, 3ᵉ, T 06 1229 9040, www.galeriegosserez.com*

S/T Concept S/Tore

The list of contributors to *Some/Things* magazine – Jarvis Cocker, Steve McQueen, Béla Tarr, Dries Van Noten, Ferran Adrià, Wong Kar-wai – reveals its progenitors' approach. They also run a creative studio and this inspiring multidisciplinary store, focusing on conceptual objects produced in collaboration with international artists and designers. We spied Pournoir's black-marble and steel 'Kundag' table, prints on aluminium from GL-OW visual arts gallery's 'Alchemy' range and a Cannondale bike (all above), as well as techie furniture by IOTA Element, ceramics from Monica Prentice, Xenophora jewellery and Mad&Len scents. The raw concrete and darkwood space also hosts events, dinners, talks, installations and exhibitions. Open by appointment. *16 villa Gaudelet, 11ᵉ, T 4700 9190, www.someslashthings.com*

Lustre Gabriel, Versailles

The monumental staircase leading to the Grands Apartments at Versailles was designed in 1772 by Louis XV's architect Ange-Jacques Gabriel, but construction came to a halt – for 200 years. Now the neoclassical austerity has been leavened by Ronan and Erwan Bouroullec's *Lustre Gabriel* chandelier: a 12m-high luminous artwork formed of three organic-looking loops of crystal and LED. The brothers from Breton worked alongside technicians at Swarovski to engineer the discreet joints and cables that allow the 800 glowing links to hang so elegantly. Versailles' protectors are said to have only given permission for the installation of a contemporary artwork in the Ancien Régime reliquary because the staircase itself is effectively new.
Palace of Versailles, T 3083 7800, www.chateauversailles.fr

Galerie Patrick Seguin

This voluminous furniture repository is owned by Patrick and Laurence Seguin. Behind a rather deceptive facade (above), remodelled in 2013, is Jean Nouvel's deft conversion of an old carpentry workshop, which has been painted white, its beams exposed, and flooded with light through a glass roof. On show are decorative pieces and furnishings by the most eminent midcentury architects and designers in France – legends including Jean Prouvé, Charlotte Perriand, Pierre Jeanneret and Le Corbusier (all represented overleaf). There is also a publishing arm, producing definitive monographs on Prouvé, and a few others. Seguin curates exhibitions at institutions such as New York's MoMA and the Vitra Design Museum in Weil am Rhein. *5 rue des Taillandiers, 11ᵉ, T 4700 3235, www.patrickseguin.com*

Gallery S Bensimon

It's all change every few months at Serge Bensimon's Marais showroom, and the vernissages are not to be missed. Themed exhibitions bring together a wide range of approaches and disciplines, from artisanal craftwork to the experimental, emanating from all over the globe. We liked the work of Canadian wood artist Brent Comber; Argentine duo Cuatro Manos Dos Cabezas; Paris-based glassblower Jeremy Maxwell Wintrebert; Brooklyn's François Chambard ('Holy Stools', opposite, behind Dan Yeffet's 'Tangram' table); and the 'Circle' chair (above), by local design studio Pool, which plays with perspective. Bensimon has a background in fashion, and the airy space, with its statement Japanese-style straw-and-earth wall, is unpretentious and fun. *111 Rue de Turenne, 3ᵉ, T 4274 5077, www.gallerybensimon.com*

Fondation Louis Vuitton

Frank Gehry's peacocking glass sails envelop 11,700 sq m of exhibition space, much of it sparsely populated, for LV billionaire Bernard Arnault to show off his art. This contentious 2014 museum rises above the treeline in the formerly protected Bois de Boulogne. A 'gift' to the city or vanity project? Time will tell.
8 avenue du Mahatma Gandhi, 16ᵉ, T 4069 9600, www.fondationlouisvuitton.fr

ARCHITOUR

A GUIDE TO THE CITY'S ICONIC BUILDINGS

There are a dozen Le Corbusier buildings in and around Paris, the city in which he lived and worked for most of his adult life. Today, some, such as Villa Besnus (85 boulevard de la République), the family home he completed in 1922 in the suburb of Vaucresson, are almost unrecognisable. Others, such as the 1951 Maisons Jaoul (81 rue de Longchamp) in verdant Neuilly-sur-Seine, which were gossip-magazine staples when they belonged to Lord Palumbo and served as a base for his friends (including Diana, Princess of Wales), have been carefully restored. Most of Le Corbusier's Paris projects are concentrated in a crescent across the southern half of the city and can be squeezed into half a day's architourism, or combined, as we suggest, with a selection of other modern gems.

Cité de Refuge (12 rue Cantagrel, 13e) is a good start. Nearby is Maison Planeix (24 bis boulevard Masséna, 13e). A house/studio, it was designed for one of Corbu's most ardent, if impecunious, clients, the sculptor Antonin Planeix. Atelier Ozenfant (53 avenue Reille, 14e) is another of the architect's live/work spaces. By the early 1930s, Le Corbusier was back in the 14th for his first public commission, Pavillon Suisse. He revisited the site for Maison du Brésil (7 boulevard Jourdan, 14e, T 5810 2300) in 1959. Fondation Le Corbusier (10 square du Docteur Blanche, 16e, T 4288 4153; closed Sundays and Monday mornings) will advise on visits.

For full addresses, see Resources.

Maison de Verre

One of the greatest houses built in the International Style is one of the least visited. Architects Pierre Chareau and Bernard Bijvoet, together with metal craftsman Louis Dalbet, worked wonders on the bones of an existing building on a small plot in the 7th arrondissement, completing the new structure in 1932. The facades are covered with glass blocks set into a steel frame, which creates a well of light while also ensuring privacy. The living room is the real show-stopper. It features steel columns with exposed bolts and thin slabs of slate, and a sliding-panel bookcase that covers one wall. Wires were threaded through metal tubing that runs from floor to ceiling. It is only open to architects, who must apply for a tour in writing; there is a six-month waiting list.
31 rue Saint-Guillaume, 7ᵉ

Fondation Jérôme Seydoux-Pathé
Renzo Piano's organic bulge in the Paris cityscape colonises the courtyard of a Haussmann-era block near Place d'Italie, an 'unexpected presence' connected to the 19th-century buildings at four points. Only a sliver of its five storeys is glimpsed over the roofline. This HQ for the Jérôme Seydoux-Pathé film foundation contains exhibition space, a 68-seater screening room, archives and offices. Entrance is via the listed 1869 facade, replete with Rodin sculptures and a glass atrium. From here, bridges lead into the curvaceous carapace of glass tiles, underpinned by timber ribs, that allows soft light into the upper levels, which are linked by a spiral staircase. Open 1pm to 7pm, Tuesday to Friday; 10am to 7pm, Saturday (€6 entry includes a film). *73 avenue des Gobelins, 13e, T 8379 1896, www.fondation-jeromeseydoux-pathe.com*

Cité de la Mode et du Design

Vivid pea-green girders and broad decks define Jakob + MacFarlane's contemporary fashion and design centre, recast from a 1907 goods depot. The new exterior is an extension of the riverside promenade and enlivens this formerly bleak area, dubbed Les Docks. L'Institut Français de la Mode is at one end and summer bar/restaurant Wanderlust (T 7074 4174), run by the Savoir Faire group (Silencio, Social Club), occupies the other. In-between are cafés, boutiques and exhibition spaces. A large expanse of grass covers the top, location of 430 sq m restaurant/bar lounge Moon Roof (T 4424 3934). The remainder of the 'skin' comprises glass and steel. Les Docks is an admirable project – whether it beds in as a true creative hub remains to be seen. *34 quai d'Austerlitz, 13ᵉ, T 7677 2530, www.citemodedesign.fr*

Communist Party Headquarters

The French Communist Party is blessed with a superlative seat from which to orchestrate its policies. Designed by architect Oscar Niemeyer (a committed communist), its HQ is one of the city's finest pieces of modernist architecture: an undulating glazed building with a series of subterranean chambers. The highlight is the sculptural conference hall, which has a white domed roof that rises in front of the pimary structure. Niemeyer collaborated with Jean Prouvé on the sinuous glass curtain wall and its mechanical window openers, and designed the furniture. Free tours can be arranged by appointment, or you may be invited to an event – Prada and Dior have rented the building for shows.
2 place du Colonel Fabien, 19ᵉ,
T 4040 1334

SHOPS

THE BEST RETAIL THERAPY AND WHAT TO BUY

At the fashion and beauty houses, radical architecture and design is vital. In 2010, Balenciaga (10 avenue George V, 8e, T 4720 2111) unveiled a spacecraft-like flagship devised by Nicolas Ghesquière and artist Dominique Gonzalez-Foerster. For its store on the Rive Gauche, Hermès (see p093) built some striking installations; and furniture design is integral to Alaïa (see p086) and Balmain (see p088). The Karl Lagerfeld boutique (194 boulevard Saint-Germain, 7e, T 4222 7499) is forcefully modern, with mobile payment devices instead of a cash desk and digital photobooths in changing rooms. And art, not bling, defines Guerlain's rebirth (see p082). For a more homespun affair, men are well catered for at knit label Monsieur Lacenaire (57 rue Charlot, 3e) and preppy brand Ami (see p084), which followed up its Marais debut with premises on the Left Bank.

The concept store was arguably born in this city (see p092), and the Colette effect is still in evidence, notably at Centre Commercial (2 rue de Marseille, 10e, T 4202 2608) and Merci (111 boulevard Beaumarchais, 3e, T 4277 0033), which is housed in an 1840 former wallpaper factory. Here you could find a jacket by Rains, a Paola Navone sofa, Cutipol cutlery and a Bindewerk notebook, with all profits going to charity. And this being Paris, there is an erudite theme to the retail landscape, in the highly browsable OFR (20 rue Dupetit-Thouars, 3e, T 4245 7288) and LO/A (see p094).

For full addresses, see Resources.

Bonastre

Sold around the world, Fernando Bonastre de Celis' vegetable-tanned leather bags and accessories now have their own space in a light-filled corner boutique. Bonastre studied in Madrid before moving to Paris to work for Christian Lacroix and Claude Montana. He created his own brand in 2011, inspired by the architecture of Tadao Ando and Oscar Niemeyer. He began with a focus on men's leather accessories; the women's line came in 2014, after the opening of the store. Bonastre describes his design ethos as 'radical purity'. Each piece, such as the document holder (above), €370, is built to last, tanned naturally using oak bark and finished in olive oil, at a family workshop in Spain. They're displayed upon a set of 100 white cubes in a monochrome space. *10 rue du Perche, 3ᵉ, T 42/8 9910, www.bonastre.net*

L'Institut Guerlain

Peter Marino, known for his boutiques for Chanel, Dior and Fendi, led the renovation of Guerlain's Champs-Élysées HQ, which was designed in 1914 by Charles Mewès, architect of the Ritz. The 1828 brand has been enshrined here in Calacatta marble, straw marquetry, a crystal-studded Proust quote, hefty Baccarat chandeliers, and an installation of inflatable golden bees. In the extension dedicated to beauty, make-up and edible delicacies, the 19,873 glassy eyes of a Norbert Brunner artwork follow you around as you browse. A white bronze orchid by Marc Quinn decorates the mezzanine, past which VIP clients are ushered to inhale rarities. On the first floor, listed Jean-Michel Frank interiors and cut onyx are deployed to heady effect (above). *68 avenue des Champs-Élysées, 8e, T 4562 1121, www.guerlain.com*

Officine Universelle Buly

You don't walk out of this store with only a Retour d'Egypte candle. Perfume matches are de rigueur, naturally, but then there are the clays for home facials, vegetable oils (certainly not the cooking kind) and, if you're not body brushing with a horsehair glove, well... Buly's products are paraben-free, and the fragrances are formulated without the use of alcohol to make them subtle and true – try the Lichen d'Ecosse, Rose de Damas or Bergamote. Defer to the knowledgeable staff, buy the house *pommade virginale*, sing along to the opera and depart happy. The gorgeous interior – a reimagining of a historic Buly *officine* inhabiting Rue Montorgueil during the 19th century – is lined with wooden cabinetry and white and turquoise tiling.
6 rue Bonaparte, 6ᵉ, 1 4329 0250, www.buly1803.com

Ami
Behind the black lacquered facade and striped awning of Ami's second boutique (the original is in the 3rd) are mirrored panels, suspended brass rails, parquet floors and a marble and oak counter. Designer Alexandre Mattiussi previously worked for Givenchy and Marc Jacobs, and his dapper menswear is hip (pattern, oversize) and dandy (linen, toile).
22 rue de Grenelle, 7ᵉ, T 09 8230 9677

Boutique Alaïa

Living legend Azzedine Alaïa called on his friends Marc Newson and Kris Ruhs to help him create this unforgettable space in a three-storey 18th-century *hôtel particulier*. Newson contributed the impressive circular light fixtures that embellish each floor, and Ruhs designed a sculptural brushed-steel chandelier for the marble staircase. Pierre Paulin pieces appear throughout, as well as two Charlotte Perriand tables and, in the courtyard (opposite), where you can take tea, Harry Bertoia chairs. The green wall here is by botanist Patrick Blanc, who pioneered the trend in Paris. Accessories are on the ground floor, and clothing is upstairs, on Martin Szekely-designed racks. The paintings by Alaïa's partner, Christoph Von Weyhe, are of the Hamburg docks. *5 rue de Marignan, 8ᵉ, 1 /672 9111, www.alaia.fr*

Balmain

The achingly elegant and graceful flagship of this Parisian fashion house whispers chic, as you might expect from Balmain. Housed in Pierre Balmain's former studio, founded in 1945, the first-floor boutique underwent a 21st-century makeover, and relaunched in 2010. The architect, Joseph Dirand, given free rein by the label's then creative director, Christophe Decarnin, restored the original cornicing, marble fireplaces and untreated Versailles parquet flooring to create a showroom for the clothes. The decoration demands as much attention as the fashion. Decarnin accented the space with furniture of his own design, a console by Gilbert Poillerat, master of wrought iron, and a table by the sculptor André Arbus.

44 rue François 1er, 8e, T 4720 3534, www.balmain.com

Nose

Nicolas Cloutier and Mark Buxton are key members of the seven-strong team that launched Nose, a 'diagnostic' perfumery offering more than a spritz of the latest couture fragrance. Instead, customers are gently quizzed about their olfactory whims and wishes before being guided towards a handful of potions that might suit. Apart from expertise and a certain sense of ceremony, what's on offer is an ahead-of-the-curve selection of scents, from Brooklyn-based DS & Durga and Dr Vranjes to Comme Des Garçons and Robert Piguet's sensational Fracas. The 175 sq m shop, replete with fridge-style storage, also stocks beauty products from Retrouvé and DR Harris, and home fragrances by Cire Trudon and Birch & Brook.
20 rue Bachaumont, 2ᵉ, T 4026 4603, www.nose.fr

Les Caves de Taillevent

André Vrinat opened the formal Taillevent restaurant back in 1946. His empire now includes a brasserie and Les Caves, which specialises in wine futures and attracts an international clientele. Since the redesign by Pierre-Yves Rochon in 2013, it occupies a pair of sleek, temperature-controlled spaces – an oak-clad *grande cave* (above) and a brick-and-steel inner sanctum that is maintained at ideal conditions for its precious contents, selected by Taillevent's enlightened sommeliers. It's not all Clos Rougeard and Domaine de la Romanée-Conti; bottles start under €10, and there are 1,500 options. Stock up here, and then, for the picnic to end them all, head to restaurant-quality deli Terroirs d'Avenir (T 4508 4880) on Rue de Nil in the 2nd. *228 rue du Faubourg Saint-Honoré, 8ᵉ, T 4561 1409, www.taillevent.com*

Galerie L'Eclaireur

Although it has been around since 1980, caters to bigwigs in fashion media and is opening in LA, L'Eclaireur can still feel like a secret destination, especially the design store that opened in the Puces at Saint-Ouen in 2013. Delights abound, from a mint 1933 American Flyer model train to Fernando and Humberto Campana's 'Cipria' sofa in gold leather and fur. The gallery provides a showcase for Milan designer Vincenzo de Cotiis' upcycled, limited-edition Progetto Domestico range. Also check out sculptural mineral lamps by the Von Pelt collective, and handmade glass one-offs by Lindsey Adelman. There is occasionally vintage designer clothing here too. Note that it only opens Saturday to Monday and on bank holidays.

77 rue des Rosiers, Puces de Saint-Ouen, T 4010 0046, www.leclaireur.com

Hermès Sèvres

After carving out its first concept store within this 1935 art deco former indoor swimming pool, Hermès turned to Rena Dumas Architecture Interieure (RDAI) to embellish the boutique. Three tall, undulating 'teepees', made from woven ash, rise 9m above the main retail floor, which shimmers with original mosaics. A fourth structure sits on the staircase that leads from the entrance level and overlooks the spectacle, its wrought-iron balconies echoing those at the Hermès HQ on Rue du Faubourg Saint-Honoré. Visit Le Plongeoir tearoom, the in-house florist Baptiste Pitou (T 4284 1908) and Chaîne d'Encre bookstore (T 4284 4157) here, before perusing the entire range of Hermès fashion and homewares.
17 rue de Sèvres, 6e, T 4222 8083, www.hermes.com

LO/A

A scholarly centre of multidisciplinary countercultural exchange, Maxime Dubois and Jeanne Holsteyn's LO/A, which stands for Library of Arts, is a bookstore and publisher that sheds its skin every six months. Set in the increasingly interesting upper fringes of the Haut-Marais, it sells books, fanzines, documents, DVDs, vinyl and ephemera, pertaining to anything from hip-hop culture to Italian graffiti; sometimes it feels more like an exhibition space than a store, always deftly curated and fresh. LO/A collaborates with festivals and other organisations too, brandishing printed matter to edify groups ranging from the techno heads at Point Ephémère (T 4034 0248) in Canal Saint-Martin to the attendees at a fashion trade show.
17 rue Notre Dame de Nazareth, 3ᵉ, T 09 8375 9108, www.libraryofarts.com

En Selle Marcel

Pedal power is ultra-cool in the capital right now. Between the foodie Montorgueil quarter and hip Saint-Denis, the superbly monikered En Selle Marcel ('On your bike, Marcel') is a boutique that caters not just for style-conscious yet wobbly Pashley types, but also for cycling connoisseurs. Vintage bikes from Schindelhauer are parked up for drooling over, Cinelli frames hang on the wall, and new breeds include Abici 1950s-inspired designs, as well as Bromptons. Rapha and Brooks are sold here, and there is clothing from Le Coq Sportif, hard-wearing manbags made by Chrome, and helmets disguised as natty green Loden caps. At the rear is a workshop, but you won't see a spot of grease on Marcel's gleaming grey floor.
40 rue Tiquetonne, 2, T 4454 0646,
www.ensellemarcel.com

ESCAPES

WHERE TO GO IF YOU WANT TO LEAVE TOWN

When they periodically abandon their city, where do Parisians go? The fact is, it's nowhere near Paris. If it's not Punta del Este or Sicily, it'll be sunny Île de Ré off La Rochelle, the leafy Limousin, or good old Provence. You ought to take advantage of the expanded TGV network, to make it to Le Havre in two hours for an Auguste Perret architour, nip to Deauville for the seafood and beaches, or make a gastro pilgrimage to La Grenouillère (see po98), just over an hour's journey from Gare du Nord via Arras. A scant two-and-a-half hours west, France's sixth-largest city, Nantes (opposite), has an outpost of the contemporary Galerie Melanie Rio (34 boulevard Guist'hau, T 02 4089 2040) among its attractions. If you head south, there's no better way to take your leave than by lingering over *un allongé* amid the overblown rococo of Le Train Bleu dining room at the Gare de Lyon (1st floor, Place Louis Armand, 12e, T 4343 0906).

Closer to home, the MAC/VAL museum (Place de la Libération, T 4391 6420), set in parkland in the south-eastern suburb of Vitry-sur-Seine, is a pleasant half-day diversion, or lose an afternoon in Le Pré Catelan restaurant (Route de Suresnes, 16e, T 4414 4114) in the Bois de Boulogne. Le Corbusier's Villa Savoye (see p102) is in Poissy, to the north-west, and the Louvre-Lens museum (see p100), a branch of the Paris institution designed by Japanese architects SANAA, is a two-hour drive north, between Amiens and Lille. *For full addresses, see Resources.*

Okko Hotels Nantes Château

The plan for this fledgling city-centre hotel chain, first unveiled in Nantes, is for nine openings across France by 2017. Designer Patrick Norguet has aimed for a luxy feel without the spend. The 80 rooms are tiny, at 18 sq m, but the comfy beds, Gastaldi linen and Nespresso machines are treats. The Club room, with its warm industrial vibe, offers 24/7 snacks included in the rate. The big idea here is that booking, checking in and paying are all digital, so there's no reception, and your mobile is your room key. There are many cultural draws in this lively former-shipbuilding city, not least the 1814 Musée des Beaux-Arts (T 02 5117 4500), whose 4,200 sq m extension by Stanton Williams, set to open in 2016, will cater for contemporary works. *15 rue de Strasbourg, T 02 5220 0070, www.okkohotels.com*

La Grenouillère, Montreuil-sur-Mer
Alexandre Gauthier, chef at this family-run restaurant since 2003, found the perfect match for his culinary creativity in architect Patrick Bouchain. Beside the original farmhouse, a pair of metal 'tents' house the dining room, which is done out in wood, burlap and leather. Eight guest chalets modelled on hunting huts are tucked away in the gardens.
Rue de la Grenouillère, T 03 2106 0722

Louvre-Lens

The selection in 2004 of the industrial Lens as host for an extension of one of the world's elite museums (the shortlist included Amiens, Boulogne-sur-Mer and Calais) screamed cultural democratisation. No mere satellite of its Paris progenitor, Louvre-Lens, opened in 2012, has been conceived to bring art to the people via multimedia tools and attendants more likely to engage you in conversation than tut at your mobile phone. Exhibits in the Glass Pavilion link with regional galleries across France; the 3,000 sq m Grande Galerie shows works from the Louvre's collection. SANAA's low steel-and-glass structures let in ample light and also reflect the surrounding landscaped park, which was built on a defunct coal mine. *99 rue Paul Bert, Lens, T 03 2118 6262, www.louvrelens.fr*

Villa Savoye, Poissy
Le Corbusier conceived Villa Savoye, the purest of his purist villas, as a 'box in the air'. He used the house's structure to orchestrate the experience of entering it, as if he were directing a film. It was completed in 1931 and stands proud in a field of straggling daisies. Don't miss it. Closed Mondays. *82 rue de Villiers, T 3965 0106, villa-savoye.monuments-nationaux.fr*

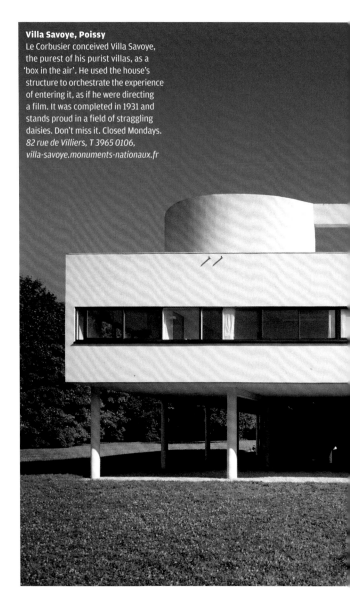

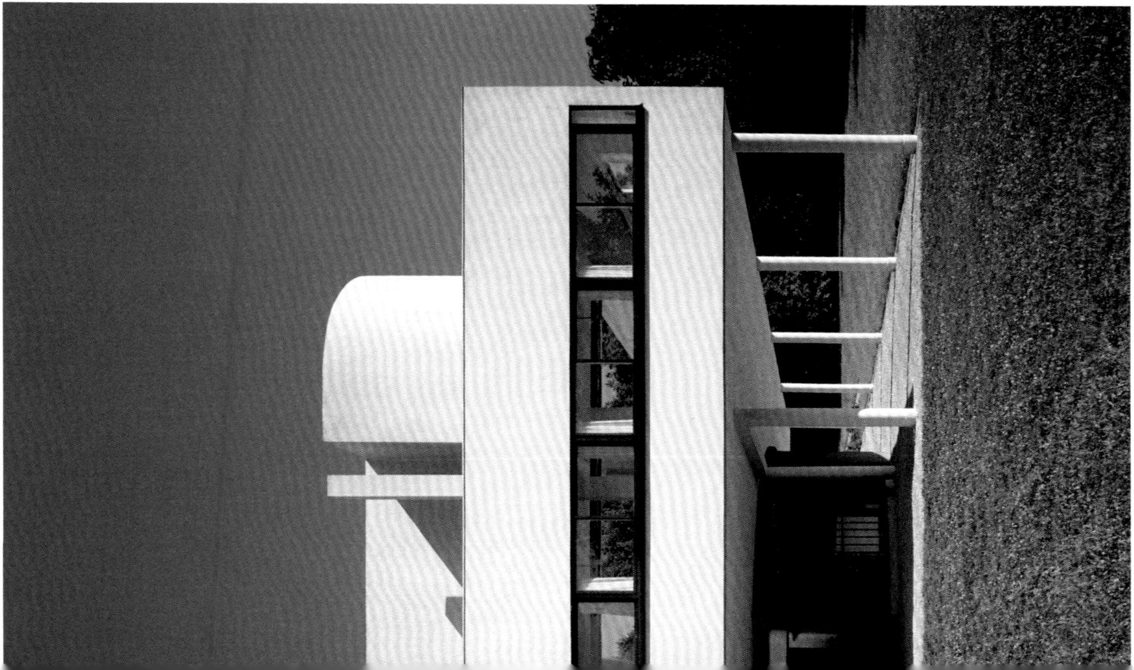

NOTES
SKETCHES AND MEMOS

RESOURCES

CITY GUIDE DIRECTORY

A

Ami 084
22 rue de Grenelle, 7ᵉ
T 09 8230 9677
www.amiparis.fr

Anahi 040
49 rue Volta, 3ᵉ
T 4887 8824
www.anahirestaurant.fr

L'Arpège 052
84 rue de Varenne, 7ᵉ
T 4705 0906
www.alain-passard.com

L'Astrance 032
4 rue Beethoven, 16ᵉ
T 4050 8440
www.astrancerestaurant.com

Atelier Ozenfant 072
53 avenue Reille, 14ᵉ
www.fondationlecorbusier.fr

Aux Deux Amis 031
45 rue Oberkampf, 11ᵉ
T 5830 3813

B

Le Bal Café 024
6 impasse de la Défense, 18ᵉ
T 4470 7551
www.le-bal.fr

Balenciaga 080
10 avenue George V, 8ᵉ
T 4720 2111
www.balenciaga.com

Balmain 088
44 rue François 1er, 8ᵉ
T 4720 3534
www.balmain.com

Baptiste Pitou 093
Hermès Sèvres
17 rue de Sèvres, 6ᵉ
T 4284 1908
www.baptistefleur.com

Le Baron 024
6 avenue Marceau, 8ᵉ
www.clublebaron.com

Le Bistrot Paul Bert 032
18 rue Paul Bert, 11ᵉ
T 4372 2401

Bonastre 081
10 rue du Perche, 3ᵉ
T 4278 9910
www.bonastre.net

Bones 030
43 rue Godefroy Cavaignac, 11ᵉ
T 09 8075 3208
www.bonesparis.com

Boutique Alaïa 086
5 rue de Marignan, 8ᵉ
T 7672 9111
www.alaia.fr

Brasserie Thoumieux 042
79 rue Saint-Dominique, 7ᵉ
T 4705 4975
www.thoumieux.com

The Broken Arm 054
12 rue Perrée, 3ᵉ
T 4461 5360
www.the-broken-arm.com

La Buvette 048
67 rue Saint-Maur, 11ᵉ
T 09 8356 9411

C

Café Artcurial 033
7 rond-point des Champs-Élysées, 8ᵉ
T 5376 3934
www.artcurial.com/cafe

Café Kitsuné 045
51 galerie de Montpensier, 1er
T 4015 6231
www.kitsune.fr

Café La Perle 054
78 rue Vieille du Temple, 3e
T 4272 6993
www.cafelaperle.com

Candelaria 054
52 rue de Saintonge, 3e
T 4274 4128
www.candelariaparis.com

Carpenters Workshop Gallery 056
54 rue de la Verrerie, 4e
T 4278 8092
www.carpentersworkshopgallery.com

Les Caves de Taillevent 090
228 rue du Faubourg Saint-Honoré, 8e
T 4561 1409
www.taillevent.com

Centre Commercial 080
2 rue de Marseille, 10e
T 4202 2608
www.centrecommercial.cc

Centre Pompidou 014
Place Georges Pompidou, 4e
T 4478 1233
www.centrepompidou.fr

Centre Pompidou-Metz 015
1 parvis des Droits-de-l'Homme
Metz
T 03 8715 3939
www.centrepompidou-metz.fr

Chaîne d'Encre 093
Hermès Sèvres
17 rue de Sèvres, 6e
T 4284 4157

Chambelland 050
14 rue Ternaux, 11e
T 4355 0730
www.chambelland.com

Le Châteaubriand 032
129 avenue Parmentier, 11e
T 4357 4595
www.lechateaubriand.com

Ciel de Paris 010
56th floor
Tour Montparnasse
33 avenue du Maine, 15e
T 4064 7764
www.cieldeparis.com

Cité de la Mode et du Design 076
34 quai d'Austerlitz, 13e
T 7677 2530
www.citemodedesign.fr

Cité de Refuge 072
12 rue Cantagrel, 13e
www.fondationlecorbusier.fr

Clamato 038
80 rue de Charonne, 11e
T 4372 7453
www.septime-charonne.fr

Clown Bar 032
114 rue Amelot, 11e
T 4355 8735

Communist Party Headquarters 078
2 place du Colonel Fabien, 19e
T 4040 1334

Compagnie des Vins Surnaturels 036
7 rue Lobineau, 6e
T 09 5490 2020
www.compagniedesvinssurnaturels.com

D

Le Dauphin 049
131 avenue Parmentier, 11^e
T 5528 7888
www.restaurantledauphin.net

Department of Islamic Art 020
Musée du Louvre
1 place du Carrousel, 1er
T 4020 5317
www.louvre.fr

Un Dimanche à Paris 024
4 cour du Commerce Saint-André, 6^e
T 5681 1818
www.un-dimanche-a-paris.com

E

L'Ecailler du Bistrot 032
22 rue Paul Bert, 11^e
T 4372 7677

Eclectic 046
2 rue Linois, 15^e
T 7736 7000
www.restauranteclectic.fr

L'Entrée des Artistes 031
8 rue de Crussol, 11^e
T 09 5099 6711

F

Flesh 032
25 rue de Douai, 9^e
T 4281 2193
www.flesh-restaurant.com

Fondation Le Corbusier 072
10 square du Docteur Blanche, 16^e
T 4288 4153
www.fondationlecorbusier.fr

Fondation Jérôme Seydoux-Pathé 074
73 avenue des Gobelins, 13^e
T 8379 1896
www.fondation-jeromeseydoux-pathe.com

Fondation Louis Vuitton 070
8 avenue du Mahatma Gandhi, 16^e
T 4069 9600
www.fondationlouisvuitton.fr

Frenchie 032
5-6 rue du Nil, 2^e
T 4039 9619
www.frenchie-restaurant.com

G

Galerie BSL 056
23 rue Charlot, 3^e
T 4478 9414
www.galeriebsl.com

Galerie L'Eclaireur 092
77 rue des Rosiers
Puces de Saint-Ouen
T 4010 0046
www.leclaireur.com

Galerie d'en Face 054
7 rue Paul-Louis Courier, 7^e
T 4439 9456
www.galeriedenface.com

Galerie Gosserez 061
3 rue Debelleyme, 3^e
T 06 1229 9040
www.galeriegosserez.com

Galerie Kreo 057
31 rue Dauphine, 6^e
T 5310 2300
www.galeriekreo.fr

Galerie Maria Wettergren 056
18 rue Guénégaud, 6^e
T 4329 1960
www.mariawettergren.com

Galerie Melanie Rio 096
34 boulevard Guist'hau
Nantes
T 02 4089 2040
www.rgalerie.com

Galerie Pascal Cuisinier 060
13 rue de Seine, 6ᵉ
T 4354 3461
www.galeriepascalcuisinier.com

Galerie Patrick Seguin 065
5 rue des Taillandiers, 11ᵉ
T 4700 3235
www.patrickseguin.com

Galerie Thaddaeus Ropac 054
69 avenue du Général Leclerc
Pantin
T 5589 0110
www.ropac.net

Gallery S Bensimon 068
111 rue de Turenne, 3ᵉ
T 4274 5077
www.gallerybensimon.com

Glass 051
7 rue Frochot, 9ᵉ
T 09 8072 9883
www.glassparis.com

Grande Arche de la Défense 011
1 parvis de la Défense

H

Hermès Sèvres 093
17 rue de Sèvres, 6ᵉ
T 4222 8083
www.hermes.com

Hôtel de Nell 053
7-9 rue du Conservatoire, 9ᵉ
T 4483 8360
www.hoteldenell.com

I

L'Institut Guerlain 082
68 avenue des Champs-Élysées, 8ᵉ
T 4562 1121
www.guerlain.com

J

La Jaja 054
56 rue d'Argout, 2ᵉ
T 09 5212 4101
www.lajaja.fr

K

Karl Largerfeld 080
194 boulevard Saint-Germain, 7ᵉ
T 4222 7499
www.karl.com

L

LiLi 017
The Peninsula
19 avenue Kléber, 16ᵉ
T 5812 6750
paris.peninsula.com

LO/A 094
17 rue Notre Dame de Nazareth, 3ᵉ
T 09 8375 9108
www.libraryofarts.com

Louvre-Lens 100
99 rue Paul Bert
Lens
T 03 2118 6262
www.louvrelens.fr

Lustre Gabriel 064
Palace of Versailles
T 3083 7800
www.chateauversailles.fr

M

Ma Cocotte 046
106 rue des Rosiers
Saint-Ouen
T 4151 7000
www.macocotte-lespuces.com

MAC/VAL 096
Place de la Libération
Vitry-sur-Seine
T 4391 6420
www.macval.fr

Maison du Brésil 072
71 boulevard Jourdan, 14ᵉ
T 5810 2300
www.maisondubresil.org

Maison Planeix 072
24 bis boulevard Masséna, 13ᵉ
www.fondationlecorbusier.fr

Maison de Verre 073
31 rue Saint-Guillaume, 7ᵉ

Maisons Jaoul 072
81 rue de Longchamp
Neuilly-sur-Seine
www.fondationlecorbusier.fr

Le Mary Celeste 051
1 rue Commines, 3ᵉ
T 09 8072 9883
www.lemaryceleste.com

Maxim's 054
3 rue Royale, 8ᵉ
T 4265 2794
www.maxims-de-paris.com

Merci 080
111 boulevard Beaumarchais, 3ᵉ
T 4277 0033
www.merci-merci.com

Monsieur Bleu 027
Palais de Tokyo
13 avenue du Président Wilson, 16ᵉ
T 4720 9047
www.monsieurbleu.com

Monsieur Lacenaire 080
57 rue Charlot, 3ᵉ
www.monsieurlacenaire.com

Moon Roof 076
Cité de la Mode et du Design
34 quai d'Austerlitz, 13ᵉ
T 4424 3934
www.moonroof.fr

Musée des Beaux-Arts 097
10 rue Georges Clemenceau
Nantes
T 02 5117 4500
www.museedesbeauxarts.nantes.fr

Musée Picasso 056
5 rue de Thorigny, 3ᵉ
T 8556 0036
www.museepicassoparis.fr

Musée du quai Branly 025
37 quai Branly, 7ᵉ
T 5661 7000
www.quaibranly.fr

N

Les Nautes 054
1 quai des Célestins, 4ᵉ
T 4274 5953
www.lesnautes.com

Nose 089
20 rue Bachaumont, 2ᵉ
T 4026 4603
www.nose.fr

O

Officine Universelle Buly 083
6 rue Bonaparte, 6ᵉ
T 4329 0250
www.buly1803.com

OFR 080
  20 rue Dupetit-Thouars, 3ᵉ
  T 4245 7288
  www.ofrsystem.com
L'Oiseau Blanc 017
  The Peninsula
  19 avenue Kléber, 16ᵉ
  T 5812 6730
  paris.peninsula.com

P
Palais de Tokyo 026
  13 avenue du Président Wilson, 16ᵉ
  T 8197 3588
  www.palaisdetokyo.com
Pamela Popo 054
  15 rue François Miron, 4ᵉ
  T 4274 1465
  www.pamelapopo.fr
Pâtisserie des Martyrs 024
  22 rue des Martyrs, 9ᵉ
  T 7118 2470
  www.sebastiengaudard.com
Pavillon Ledoyen 032
  Carré des Champs-Élysées
  8 avenue Dutuit, 8ᵉ
  T 5305 1001
  www.yannick-alleno.com
Le Perchoir 031
  14 rue Crespin du Gast, 11ᵉ
  T 4806 1848
  www.leperchoir.fr
Point Ephémère 094
  200 quai de Valmy, 10ᵉ
  T 4034 0248
  www.pointephemere.org

Le Pré Catelan 096
  Route de Suresnes, 16ᵉ
  Bois de Boulogne
  T 4414 4114
  www.restaurant-precatelan.com

R
Roseval 047
  1 rue d'Eupatoria, 20ᵉ
  T 09 5356 2414
  www.roseval.fr

S
Le 6 Paul Bert 041
  6 rue Paul Bert, 11ᵉ
  T 4379 1432
Saturne 039
  17 rue Notre-Dame des Victoires, 2ᵉ
  T 4260 3190
  www.saturne-paris.fr
En Selle Marcel 095
  40 rue Tiquetonne, 2ᵉ
  T 4454 0646
  www.ensellemarcel.com
Septime 052
  80 rue de Charonne, 11ᵉ
  T 4367 3829
  www.septime-charonne.fr
Le Sergent Recruteur 034
  41 rue Saint-Louis en l'Île, 4ᵉ
  T 4354 7542
  www.lesergentrecruteur.fr
Le Servan 032
  32 rue Saint-Maur, 11ᵉ
  T 5528 5182
  www.leservan.com
Silencio 054
  142 rue Montmartre, 2ᵉ
  www.silencio-club.com

SÔMA 032
13 rue de Saintonge, 3e
T 09 8181 5351
S/T Concept S/Tore 062
16 villa Gaudelet, 11e
T 4700 9190
www.someslashthings.com
Stern Caffè 044
47 passage des Panoramas, 2e
T 7543 6310
www.caffestern.com
The Sunken Chip 047
39 rue des Vinaigriers, 10e
T 5326 7446
www.thesunkenchip.com

T
13 Bonaparte 054
2 bis rue de Normandie, 3e
T 4271 8315
www.13bonaparte.com
Terroirs d'Avenir 090
6-8 rue de Nil, 2e
T 4508 4880
Tour Montparnasse 010
33 avenue du Maine, 15e
T 4538 5256
www.tourmontparnasse56.com
Le Train Bleu 096
Gare de Lyon
1st floor
Place Louis Armand, 12e
T 4343 0906
Triode 056
28 rue Jacob, 6e
T 4329 4005
www.triodedesign.com

U
UNESCO Headquarters 012
7 place de Fontenoy, 7e
www.unesco.org

V
Vallois 058
36 rue de Seine, 6e
T 4634 6107
www.galerie-vallois.com
Villa Besnus 072
85 boulevard de la République
Vaucresson
www.fondationlecorbusier.fr
Villa Savoye 102
82 rue de Villiers
Poissy
T 3965 0106
villa-savoye.monuments-nationaux.fr

W
Wanderlust 076
Cité de la Mode et du Design
32 quai d'Austerlitz, 13e
T 7074 4174
www.wanderlustparis.com

WALLPAPER* CITY GUIDES

Executive Editor
Jeremy Case

Author
Sophie Dening

Art Editor
Eriko Shimazaki

Photography Editor
Elisa Merlo
Assistant Photography Editor
Nabil Butt

Editorial Assistant
Emilee Jane Tombs

Sub-Editor
Nick Mee

Intern
Capucine Coninx

Production Controller
Sophie Kullmann

Original Design
Loran Stosskopf
Map Illustrator
Russell Bell

Wallpaper* ® is a
registered trademark
of IPC Media Limited

First published 2006
Revised and updated
2008, 2009, 2010, 2011,
2013 and 2014
Eighth edition 2015

© Phaidon Press Limited

All prices and venue
information are correct at
time of going to press,
but are subject to change.

Contacts
wcg@phaidon.com
@wallpaperguides

More City Guides
www.phaidon.com/travel

Phaidon Press Limited
Regent's Wharf
All Saints Street
London N1 9PA

Phaidon Press Inc
65 Bleecker Street
New York, NY 10012

Phaidon® is a registered
trademark of Phaidon
Press Limited

www.phaidon.com

A CIP Catalogue record for
this book is available from
the British Library.

Printed in China

ISBN 978 0 7148 6851 6

PHOTOGRAPHERS

Pol Baril
L'Institut Guerlain, p082

Nicolas Borel
Cité de la Mode et du
Design, pp076-077

Studio Bouroullec
Lustre Gabriel, p064

Marcin Brzezicki
Maison de Verre, p073

Raffaele Cipolletta
Louvre Department of
Islamic Art, pp028-029

Michel Denancé
Fondation Jérôme
Seydoux-Pathé, p074
Hermès Sèvres, p093

Adrien Dirand
Hôtel Paradis, p018
Monsieur Bleu, p027
Le Sergent Recruteur,
p034, p035
Le 6 Paul Bert, p041
Roseval, p047
La Buvette, pp048-049
Hôtel de Nell, p053
Balmain, p088

Todd Eberle
Fondation Louis Vuitton,
pp070-071

Julien Fernandez
Paris city view,
inside front cover
The Peninsula, p017
Bones, p030
Le Perchoir, p031
Clamato, p038
Anahi, p040
Stern Caffè, p044
Café Kitsuné, p045
Eclectic, p046
Chambelland, p050
Le Mary Celeste, p051
Alpha Sidibe, p055
Galerie Pascal
Cuisinier, p060
S/T Concept S/Tore,
p062, p063
Gallery S Bensimon, p068
Fondation Jérôme
Seydoux-Pathé, p075
Officine Universelle Buly,
p083
Ami, pp084-085
Boutique Alaïa, p086,
p087
Les Caves de Taillevent,
pp090-091
Galerie L'Eclaireur, p092
LO/A, p094

Eric Forlini
En Selle Marcel, p095

Jérôme Galland
Saturne, p039
Galerie Gosserez, p061
Okko Hotels Nantes
Château, p097

Clément Guillaume
Compagnie des Vins
Surnaturels, pp036-037
Septime, p052
Galerie Kreo, p057
Communist Party
Headquarters, pp078-079
Nose, p089

Alex Hill
Hôtel Particulier
Montmartre, p023
Musée du quai
Branly, p025

Hotelexistence.com
Grande Arche de la
Défense, p011
UNESCO Headquarters,
pp012-013

**Hotelexistence.com
(FLC/ADAGP, Paris and
DACS London 2012)**
Villa Savoye, pp102-103

Florent Michel
Palais de Tokyo, p026

Emile Ouroumov
Vallois, pp058-059

Jacques Pépion
Café Artcurial, p033

Ildiko Peter
La Grenouillère,
pp098-099

James Reeve
Hôtel Particulier
Montmartre, p022
Brasserie Thoumieux,
pp042-043

Patrick Seguin Gallery
Galerie Patrick Seguin,
p065, pp066-067

Hisao Suzuki
Louvre-Lens, pp100-101

Gilles Trillard
Hotel Molitor, p020

Sebastien Veronese
Hôtel Jules & Jim, p019

PARIS
A COLOUR-CODED GUIDE TO THE CITY'S HOT 'HOODS

MONTMARTRE
The hill is home to the *haute* bourgeoisie; at its foot is the city's (reformed) sin central

CANAL SAINT-MARTIN
Alongside this canal in the 10th arrondissement, east-Paris hipsters set up shop and play

CHAMPS-ÉLYSÉES
Les Champs will always be touristy, but the area around it is full of stylish destinations

RÉPUBLIQUE/BASTILLE
It's still youthful but more polished these days, thanks to a shot of *bon chic, bon genre*

MARAIS
These streets were made for strolling. Galleries, boutiques, bars, bistros – take your pick

BEAUBOURG/LOUVRE
Come here for art and architecture that is impossible to miss and still apt to inspire

SAINT-GERMAIN-DES-PRÉS/QUARTIER LATIN
Sartre and de Beauvoir's Left Bank stomping ground is more about retail these days

LES INVALIDES
Among the many monuments here is now another fine prize – Jean Nouvel's museum

For a full description of each neighbourhood, see the Introduction.
Featured venues are colour-coded, according to the district in which they are located.